Goodnight, Loon:

Poems and Parodies
To Survive the Trump Presidency

By: Howard B. Altman

Dedication

This is for my parents, Stewart and Emily Altman, who gave me the values to stand up for equality, and who filled my life with laugher, wisdom, and music. Thank you for all your encouragement, support and love, and for never yelling at me for coloring outside the lines, even that time I drew on my bedroom wall to try and make it look like The Gong Show. Sorry about that!

Introduction

Donald Trump is an ignorant, arrogant, racist, witless, heartless, hopeless, narcissistic, nihilistic, vulgar, vile, hate-spewing, press-attacking, Nazi-loving, Hillary-obsessed, tiny-handed, orange-tinted moron.

So, I began writing parodies and poems, because if I did not laugh at it all, I might have cried. This is for all of you who laughed with me. Or at me. Or in my general vicinity. Thank you.

A note on content: This is a 50-50 mix of parodies and poems. If prefaced by "Song Break", sing along (preferably aloud!) to the song parodied. Otherwise, it's a poem, and you can add your own music! It's fun!

A note on formatting: Lyrics/poems are mine. Typos are Siri's.

An Opening Limerick

There once was a moron named Trump
Whose tweets proved him dumb as a stump.
We'll all be delighted
When he is indicted.
And tossed on his fat, orange rump.

Christmas Carols

It's Beginning to Look a lot like Treason
(To It's Beginning to Look a lot Like Christmas)

It's beginning to look a lot like treason
Everywhere you go.
There's a Russian behind the Prez
Controlling what he says
Indictments falling like a Moscow snow.

It's beginning to look a lot like treason.
Mueller will not fail.
Oh what a sight to see
The MAGA morons flee
As he's put in jail.

Come All Ye Felons
(To Come All Ye Faithful)

Come all ye felons, spill your guts to Mueller.
Come ye, o come ye, and rat on your boss.
Strike a plea bargain.
Save your own skin while you can.
Oh how we abhor him.
We really do deplore him.
We'd be so thankful for him
If he would resign.

Headline: Don Jr. releases copies of his emails in which he agreed to meet with Russian agents at Trump Tower to get dirt on Hillary Clinton.

To The Dreidel Song

It's clear that he colluded
And Muller's closing in
FoxNews-ers are deluded
Treason is a sin.

Oh Fredo, Fredo Fredo
And all of Putin's men
Will never make the "nice" list
It's Christmas in the Pen.

Roy Moore's Winter Wonderland

Told the world he's a Christian.
But for kids he's been itchin'.
He lies and he hates.
Takes children on dates.
One more thing Roy doesn't understand.

Voters spoke, we all heard it.
But Roy don't like the verdict.
He isn't a judge.
He's holding a grudge.
One more thing he doesn't understand.

One fine day a doctor will sedate him.
He may hem and haw, and he may chafe.
But when he is under they'll castrate him.
And finally all the kiddies will be safe.

Adios, Roy we'll see ya'.
You are like gonorrhea.
Just go away
Each of us pray.
One more thing that you don't understand.

Poems for Pundits

Ode to Hannity

I do not like Sean Hannity.
Raving in insanity.
Bane all to humanity.
Spouting his profanity.
Faking Christianity.
Morally an absentee.
Lies for all the world to see.
One day of him we'll all be free.

Ode to Not-a-Judge Jeannine Pirro

I think that I have never seen
A shill like not-a-judge Jeannine.
Stalking Hillary in the woods.
As her fans don their Klan hoods.
She claims that she's for law and order.
She has a mental health disorder.
Jeannine, with your speeding ticket
I'd to tell you where to stick it.

Ode to Tomi Lahren

Ptomaine Lahren, what a fright.
Claimed "you hate me cause I'm white!"
Tomi's really quite the winner.
Munching on Tide Pods for dinner.
For, she heard they make you whiter.
And, of course, that did delight her.
Seems the bleach her hair retained
Leached too much into her brain.

Song break! Desperate Donald
(To The Eagles' Desperado)

Desperate Donald
Why don't you come to your senses?
You're out of defenses, the Feds closing in.
You're a moron, we know you're guilty of treason.
We all know the reason: you're guilty as sin.

I know you say you're fine, boy.
You're a genius and you're stable.
But we all know you're anything but bright.
Spending all your hours
Watching FOX&Friends on cable.
I doubt you ever learned to read or write.

Desperate Donald at least you still have Scott Baio.
Tell him hold the mayo when he rings up your food.
You're still a moron.
But maybe someone can teach you.
They're gonna impeach you,
Oh Donnie you're screwed.

Stanza for Stormy Daniels

Goodnight Twitter, Don the Liar
Mueller, who you tried to fire.
Goodnight, Stormy, who has seen
Trump spanked with a magazine.
Goodnight, Melania, too, of course.
Clean him out in your divorce.

Song Break: To The Addams Family Theme

His classless & he's gaudy.
He wants Ivanka's body.
With Russia he's been naughty.
The Trump crime family
da da da dum (snap snap)

Of course they all colluded.
Donnie is deluded.
They should all be booted.
The Trump crime family.

Part 2: For Sarah Huckabee

She's creepy and she's scummy.
A homophobic dummy.
With Trumpers she is chummy.
Sara Huckabee da da da dum (snap snap)

She lets the hatred fester.
Endorsed child molester.
I really do detest her.
Sara Huckabee.

: Trump prepares for his first State of the Union ("SOTU") Address.

January 28, 2018

Many will likely feel nauseous or squirm
At the SOTU address for the fat moron's term.
You can bet if he stays on his message at all
He'll rant about Hillary and beg for a wall.
I'm sure his musings will be a blast:
As instead of a future, he begs for the past.
Hey Donnie, we get it: Nostalgia looms large.
We wish that Obama still was in charge.

For Paul Nehlen and the other "nationalists"

Goodnight, Twitter, goodnight moon.
Goodnight Nunes, treason goon.
Night, Paul Nehlen, Nazi scum.
Shove a cactus up your bum.
Tomi, with your awful weave,
Take your racist crap and leave.
Tomorrow, do an act of grace:
Punch a Nazi in the face.

Song Break: To Paul Simon's The Boxer

I am just a dullard, and my rants are getting old.
I'm have squandered my inheritance
On a handful of failed ventures
Like Trump Magazine.
I am a mess.
But my base hears what it wants to hear
And disregards the rest.

When I gave some jobs to my family
No one else would they employ.
I surround myself with yes-men
And I tune TV to FoxNews station,
Running off, Mar-a-Lago.
Seeking out the brain dead viewers
Tuned to Tomi Lahren's show.
As they bask in the warmth of my orange glow.
Lie, lie, lie
Lie, lie, lie, lie, lie, lie, lie.
Lie, lie, lie.
All Don knows how to do is tweet and lie.

February 2, 2018

Headline: The GOP releases the "Nunes Memo" alleging wrongdoing by the FBI. Devin Nunes, Matt Gaetz and Seb Gorka take to FoxNews to claim the Russia probe is illegal.

For Devin Nunes's famed memo

Goodnight Twitter, g'night moon.
Gulag, Trump will see you soon.
Goodnight Nunes, Putin's stooge.
You epic fail at subterfuge.
The dossier wasn't used, you see.
The info: Papadoplous plea.
For all the lies you did employ.
You failed bigly, Rat-faced boy.
Matt Gaetz slurring on FoxNews.
Even here I smell the booze.
Gorka you dumb Nazi git,
Go choke on your tourniquet.
Nunes, man, your memo sucked.
Now all know Don did obstruct.

Song Break: To Gilbert & Sullivan's Modern Major General

I am the very model of raging orange narcissist.
I rant about Binomo, a country that does not exist.
I lack in basic knowledge
Things linguistic and grammatical.
But I spout Nazi rhetoric,
My views are quite fanatical.

The drivel on my twitter feed,
Like diarrhea never ends.
I know I am the smartest Prez
I just heard it on Fox&Friends.
I know all the bigly words & claim to be a brainiac.
But really I'm a moron and a raving megalomaniac.

I do not know the meaning
Of decorum or diplomacy.
I'm guilty of treason, money laundering, conspiracy.
In short, in matters literary, history and sensical
I am the very model of a tiny orange genital.

For Trump's Claim that the Nunes Memo Exonerated him

Goodnight Twitter, goodnight moon.
Goodnight orange, fat baboon.
The memo sought transparency?
Then when will we your taxes see?
Treason best viewed through the lens
Of all the lies on Fox&Friends.
Band of thieves, goodnight to thee
Tide Pod nation, GOP.
Nazi Miller, moron Trump
How is all that "winning", chump?
The Dow has tanked. The memo dud,
That dropped with a resounding thud.
Yet still you tweet that all is fine.
The tweet we'd like? "I, Trump, resign."

Nunes, though you tried to lie
You only helped the FBI.
The memo helped to validate
The Russia probe you clearly hate.
Nunes, Sara, Don, distort
But soon we'll see you all in court.

Song Break! Odes to Roy Moore After Alabama's Special Election

Democrat Doug Jones is elected in Alabama's Special Election after allegations that Roy Moore had inappropriate contact with one or more minors.

To Frosty the Snowman

Roy Moore the bigot
Tried to steal the Senate race.
But he's just a vile
Hateful pedophile
So he lost big in disgrace.

Roy Moore the bigot
Is an anti-Semite fool.
So despised, should be circumcised
With a dull & rusty tool.

There must have been some magic
In Trump's endorsement tweet.
For when I woke on this great morn
Jones had won the Senate seat.

Oh, Roy More the bigot
10 Commandments he loves well.
It was all a heist, he's the antichrist.
I am sure he'll rot in hell.

Jingle Bells for Roy Moore

Scoping out the malls.
Looking for some dates.
Staring at preteens,
While he masturbates.

Oh! Rot in hell, rot in hell!
Bible-thumping ape.
It's not a "date" when they're 14
It's statutory rape.

To Hey Jude

Roy Moore, you stupid cad.
Alabama just had a vision.
Rejected your tired litany of hate.
Now make a date for circumcision.

Hey Roy, don't take it bad.
They can vote now, those kids you dated.
You're lucky to get away with a loss.
If I was boss
You'd be castrated.

February 7, 2018

Headline: Trump demands his own military parade and claims that it's treason not to clap for him during the State of the Union address.

Ode to Orange Rocket Man

Goodnight Trump, you balding loon.
Do you think you're Kim Jung Un?
You now demand your own parade?
Your whole term's been one charade.
You love to brag about your wealth?
Want a parade? Go fund yourself.
As for your wall, the Dow just tanked.
So shove your wall where you were spanked.
You say it's treason not to clap?
Shut your flapping orange trap.
I'll clap the day that you resign.
So stick it where the sun don't shine.

Song Break! To the Beverly Hillbillies Theme

Come listen to a story bout a man named Trump
Rich white trash & he's dumber than a stump.
KFC & Big Macs all he lives on for his food.
Do they serve it in prison, cause Donnie did collude
Treason that is, conspiracy.

Well the first thing you know
Ol Trump is in the Pen.
Convicted of conspiracy by 12 women & men.
Finally then America will once again be free.
Incarcerate old Don he committed felony.

February 8, 2018

Ode to Rob Porter

Trump the raging tweeting loon.
Promised he'd drain the lagoon.
Every hire, each supporter
Is like scummy Rob Porter.
Every one that Trump invited
Felons, crooks, the lot indicted.
Racist fools of morals barren.
Nazi Gorka, sloppy Bannon.
Donnie it is time to panic.
Your admin is like The Titanic.
Rant each day about the border.
Yet no word about Rob Porter.
Your "build a wall" line's getting tired.
The real thugs are the guys you hired.
Lendowski, Porter & the rest
Your staff of degenerates.
I'd take MX any day
Over the crap that you array.

Song Break! To Genesis's Land of Confusion
(Co-written with Sam Kirkman a/k/a @PolitiSass)

He must have sent 1000 tweets.
Watched hookers peeing on the sheets.
But Mueller's probe will set things right.
And Donny, they will indict.

He tweeted "its fake news" today.
But we were not born yesterday.
For when the probe's conclusion's reached.
Donnie, you'll be impeached.

There's so many lies.
So many tantrums.
There are many deceptions.
And not much truth goin' 'round.
Can't you see
These are your crimes of collusion.

Whatever dream you live in.
Donny, you're going to prison.
Give up and just stop lying.
Donny, your term will soon be through.
At this point it's a given.
Donny, you're going to prison.
There's not point in you denying
Prison is where you're going to.

And this is the hell we live in.
We flat-out refuse to give in
We're going to stand up to you
Cause justice is still worth fighting for.

February 10, 2018

<u>Headline</u>: Trump blocks the release of the
Democrat's rebuttal memo and refuses to
implement sanctions against Russia.

MemoGate

Goodnight Twitter goodnight rain.
If only Trump had half a brain.
Blocking sanctions? Not too subtle.
Nunez memo, block rebuttal.
Don, you're guilty. Each act shows it.
Even Sloppy Bannon knows it.
Mueller will give you a bootin'
And you can crawl right back to Putin.

<u>Headline</u>: A preview of Fire & Fury is released, including an excerpt in which Steve Bannon called Don Jr.'s meeting with Russians "treasonous".

Song Break! Deep State, to Aerosmith's Rag Doll

"Deep State", Trump is busy tweetin'.
"It's fake", his followers are bleatin'.
But soon Mueller will be knocking on the back door.
Oh no, The Fire & The Fury!
Who's Steve? My memory is blurry.
Bannon, the coffee boy I never ever met before.

February 11, 2018

<u>Headline</u>: Paul Nehlen, who is running for Senate as a white Nationalist and vocal anti-Semite, was banned from Twitter after a racist tweet about Meghan Markel.

He Did Nazi That Coming

Twitter's down one Nazi goon.
Banned is Nehlen, none too soon.
Finally Twitter shut his trap.
And stopped his anti-Semite crap.
His hateful, racist, vile views
His cosplay Nixon "list of Jews".
Trump may think that Paul's just fine,
But Nehlen's lowly Nazi swine.

February 14, 2018

Goodnight Twitter, pals of mine.
Hope you had nice Valentines.
Why they love Trump, all the born again?
When he cheats with stars of porn again.
He cries, "Ivanka won't adore me.
So I'll bed her proxy, Stormy"
Hope your Valentines is better.
Except Don Jr., the bed wetter.

February 15, 2018

Roses are red, violets bore me.
Trump's valentine this year will be Stormy.
How many wives did orange-utan cheat on?
How many porn stars is tiny hands sweet on?
Donnie will try, come hell or high water
To bed every lady who looks like his daughter.
What will Melania do of course?
Run & file for divorce.

February 16, 2018

<u>Headline</u>: Trump, after reports that numerous associates said he was stupid and mentally unstable, tweeted that he was "like, very smart, a genius, even, and a stable genius at that."

Song Break: To Total Eclipse of the Heart

People say I'm dumb and I'm losing my mind.
And I'm really falling apart.
But it's fake news, cause I'm like totally smart.
They say I sit & tweet, KFC in my hand.
That I am a pawn to Breitbart.
But it's fake news cause I'm like totally smart.

February 16, 2018

<u>Headline</u>: Robert Mueller announces numerous
indictments in the Russia election meddling probe.

Goodnight Twitter much excitement.
Counting all the new indictments.
Can't wait for the repercussions.
As all the Trumps collude with Russians.
Let's send them our thoughts and prayers.
They will be caught unawares.
For now Mueller has the reason.
To indict them all for treason.

Song Break! To the Mickey Mouse Theme

Who's the scumbag predator
Disgusting as can be?
D O N A L D   T R U M P!
Who will grab your p--sy
And harass unless you flee?
D O N A L D   T R U M P!

February 18, 2018

<u>Headline</u>: The NRA lashes out at the Parkland
students, who seek common sense gun laws after 17
children are murdered by a student armed with an
AR-15.

Goodnight Twitter g'night moon.
GOP you'll be out soon.
Travel bans & border walls --
Brown skin kills, & duty calls.
But white guys with AR15s--
We see what complicit means.
All life matters, you all say.
It doesn't to the NRA.
I say no more, no more may kill.
If you won't act, then voters will.

Another Ode to the NRA

Hello Twitter, what to say?
God, I hate the NRA.
Vile, crazy Dana Loesch.
Shrill, psychotic, rich white trash.
Jail you, Dana, I'm all for it.
Your gun? I know where you can store it.
Where no trace of sun remains.
In short, where you keep your brains.

February 19, 2018 President's Day

Goodnight Twitter, what to say
As we end this Prez's Day?
Hope it all gets better, maybe
Than this fat & whiny baby.
"It's all deep state, no collusion!"
Whines the king of all delusion.
I bet each campaign discussion.
Was translated into Russian.
Come on Mueller and be fast.
Indict his 300-lb ass.

Song Break: A Few of Their Favorite Things
(To a Few of My Favorite Things)

Tax cuts for mansions and solid gold potties.
Tax cuts for Bentleys and new Masaratis.
Torturing kittens, removing flies' wings.
These are the GOP's favorite things.

Ignorant comments about foreign powers.
Paid Russian hookers who give golden showers.
Laundering money to pull corporate strings.
These are the dotard's favorite things.

But her emails! No collusion! All that he can say.
I wish he'd just take his favorite things
And go the heck away.

Ode to Sara Huckabee

Lies are all that she can say.
While her eyebrows run away.
Sara Sanders, you're infernal.
Are you related to the Colonel?
KFC's the only reason.
You'd be kept on by Capt. Treason.

February 21, 2018

<u>Headline</u>: Right wing talking head Dinesh Dsouza
says the Parkland kids are FBI plants making it all
up for attention.

Goodnight Twitter g'night moon.
D. DSouza vile goon.
Blame the kids & say they lie?
They're plants of the FBI?
Dinesh for all your crazy yellin'
You are nothing but a felon.
Felons cannot own a gun
So take your rage and stow it, hon.

Song Break! The Ballad of Joe Arpaio
(To the Ballad of Davey Crocket/The Davey
Crocket Theme)

Joe is the poster boy for bigotry.
Called Obama's birth record a forgery.
Flouted the law, hated equality.
Then was convicted of a felony.*
Joey, Joe Arpaio Clown of the Wild Frontier.

* Poetic license: Actually, he was convicted of a
misdemeanor (contempt of court), not a felony, but
felony rhymed.

February 22, 2018

<u>Headline</u>: NRA says its freedom is being attacked
by the Parkland students.

Goodnight people everywhere.
Go to hell Wayne LaPierre.
You allege conspiracy
To stop you all from being free.
We want freedom from the slaughter
Of every son and every daughter.
F your guns you terrorist.
We want freedom to exist.
Death & lies is all you sell.
NRA can go to hell.

February 23, 2018

Couplet for CPAC
CPAC spewing the same drama.
Attacking Hillary and Obama.
The "lock her up" crap Don incited?
It's his staff that's been indicted.
All know Don is just a slob.
Awful at his current job.
Donny this one thing is true:
The one to be locked up is you.

February 24, 2018

<u>Headline</u>: In a speech at CPAC, NRA spokeswoman
Dana Loesch rails against any restriction on gun
sales. Addressing the recent school shootings, she
shrugged, and said "grieving white mothers are
ratings gold." Literally. That is not a joke. She said
that. A series of her tweets found her boasting of
skinning squirrels alive "as a lesson to others", and
opining that it should be legal to assault someone
who cut you off in traffic. Because those are stable
statements from someone who should have an
assault weapon…

Ode to Dana Loesch

Goodnight Twitter g'night moon.
Dana Loesch's an effing loon.
Dana's unlike other girls.
Likes to boast of skinning squirrels.
Said gun deaths are "ratings gold".
It seems as if her soul was sold.
Dana oh so cruel crass,
Shove your rifle up your a$$.

Thoughts and Prayers for the NRA

Goodnight Twitter g'night moon.
NRA it's your high noon.
Vile Loesch & LaPierre,
Here is our one thought & prayer:
These brave FL boys & girls
Will stop you, Dana, like your squirrels.
These kids, they are not done with you.
Your reign of terror will be through.

Song break! To Tom Petty's American Girl
Dedicated to Dana Loesch

She had an obsession with squirrels.
Saw them everywhere.
Tweeted that she skins them live.
Dana Loesch needs mental help.
After all she is a psychopath.
Lots of people she threatened.
And if she ever snaps, we will say:
You had to see it coming NRA.
Oh yeah, all right.
She's a lunatic, and her mind's not right.
Dana likes to terrorize squirrels.

February 26, 2018

<u>Headline</u>: Trump blasts Florida guards for failing to enter Parkland's Marjorie Stoneman Douglas High School, and claims he'd have run into the school unarmed to stop the shooter.

Ode to the Toupeed Cowboy

Goodnight Twitter, g'night moon.
Trump, my G-d, you're a maroon.
You'd run into the school unarmed?
Dr. Ronny'd be alarmed.
With that gut & derriere
You're not running anywhere.
Capt. Bone Spurs, soft like Jell-O.
No hero, just orange-yellow.
The only running you will do
Is fleeing from Muller's Qs.

February 28, 2018

<u>Headline</u>: Hope Hicks resigns.

The White House has Lost All Hope

Goodnight Twitter, g'night moon.
Looks as Hope will be out soon.
Hicks who'd run at any minute
To press Trumps pants with him still in it.
Dated Trump & then Rob Porter
Who could bring the same disorder?
Her replacement sure won't bore me.
Trump'll probably hire Stormy.

Song Break. To The Beatles A Day in the Life

I saw FoxNews today, oh boy.
A man with skin like orange marmalade.
And though he tweeted he was #SAD.
He'd fail a polygraph. He is a psychopath.

He is beholden to a tsar.
His twitter meltdowns have been getting strange.
But Mueller's team all clearly cared.
They'd seen this case before.
Nobody is really sure of
All the crimes he's guilty for.
I'd love to jail you Don......

March 2, 2018:

Headline: It's Dr Seuss Day!

If I was the dotard, I'd sit and I'd tweet
From the comforty comfort of my gold toilet seat.
I'd tweet "Crooked Hillary!"
I'd tweet "it's Fake News!"
I'd tweet to Matt Gaetz who is reeking of booze.
I'd tweet "I love Putin", say "Nazis are fine".
But the best tweet of all: "USA, I resign."

I do not like the MAGA sham.
I do not like it Sam I Am.
I do not like the Russian trolls.
Meddling election polls.
Gun attacks without a reason.
Orange fools committing treason.
I hope that Mueller does not fail.
To put the bumbling fool in jail.

March 3, 2018:

<u>Headline</u>: Roy Moore claims to be broke from
lawsuits, and begs for donations:

Shout it from the vales and hills.
Roy Moore cannot pay his bills.
Says he cannot make ends meet.
Also can't accept defeat.
Blames LBGT, Blacks & Jews
For joining forces in their views.
Views that we the people shape
Equal rights, no child rape.
Sorry Roy, that you're not well.
No I'm not, Roy, go to hell.

Goodnight gal & g'night bloke.
God I love that Roy Moore's broke.
Begging Facebook for donations.
Just more of his machinations.
Rails against LGBT.
And against the Jews like me.
Roy, you're lacking mental health.
Pay your bills? Go fund yourself.

Song Break: To The Who's Pinball Wizard

Ever since he was elected, an embarrassment to all.
Speaks like a 2nd grader, his hands are just as small.
Obsesses over Hillary, and rants about his wall.
That dumb racist dotard just might doom us all.
He's an orange dotard, his hair & skin are bleached.
An orange dotard let's hope that he's impeached.

March 4, 2018:

Headline: NRA TV's Dana Loesch releases a video threatening the media, Hollywood and athletes.

Gather Twitter, all my tweeps.
Dana Loesch gives me the creeps.
See her threatening video now?
Jail the psychopathic cow.
All of us should be set free.
Of threats from NRATV.
Vile Dana, take your guns
And shove them up your pale white buns.
Though some may find crass.
Dana blow it out your a$$.

March 5 2018,

<u>Headline</u>: Matt Gaetz, king of the DUI's, again takes to FauxNews to criticize the Russia investigation.

Gather closely Twitter mates.
Hear the tale of drunk Matt Gaetz.
7 DUI frat boy mess
Should not be in our Congress.
See him slurring on FoxNews?
Still drunk & reeking of booze.
Talking up his buddy Trump
He should be out on his rump.
When they put Matt in the clink
He'll still want to bum a drink.

March 6, 2018:

<u>Headline</u>: Dana Loesch is at it again, this time releasing a pre-Oscars video threatening actors.

Goodnight Twitter, tweeps so kind.
Dana Loesch has lost her mind.
Clings to her AR15
Dana needs some Thorazine.
Vile, angry, shrill banshee
Rants on NRATV.
One who thinks assault is fun
Should not be let near a gun.
FBI, please heed our plea
Lest she go on a killing spree.

March 7, 2018

<u>Headline</u>: Stormy Daniels sues to get out of a non-disclosure agreement with "David Dennision" a/k/a Trump.

Hello Twitter, what a hoot!
Seems like Stormy's filed suit.
Says she has some pics to share
Show Don's orange everywhere.
Will the fact that Stormy's suing
Finally be the Don's undoing?
She could post a proving pic
But all it'd do was make us sick.
Flaccid, wrinkled, orange, tiny.
Photos of Fat Mussolini.
He'd still tweet that it's fake news.
And we? There'd be a lunch to lose.

March 8, 2018: Martin Sklerel sentenced to 7 years in prison.

Pharma Bro facing his deepest of fears
Sentenced to jail for 7 years.
Oh, poor Marty what can I can say?
Trump would have picked you for the FDA.
Give up appeals, give up all hope.
And Marty, advice: don't drop the soap.

March 9, 2018:

<u>Headline</u>: NRA sues to block a new Florida law that
would raise the age to buy assault weapons to 21.

NRA thinks it'd be fun
If every child had a gun.
Now they say you cannot stifle
Kids who want an auto rifle.
16? Felon? Crazy, ill?
Have an Uzi, time to kill.
Let the victims cry & holler,
Lobby's gotta make a dollar.
NRA, you greedy swine
Stick it where the sun don't shine.

March 10, 2018.

: Kellyanne Conway found to have
violated the Hatch Act by endorsing Roy Moore on
the news.

Goodnight Twitter g'night moon.
Kellyanne the shriveled prune
Broke the Hatch Act pushing Moore.
And she has more fun in store.
Numberg's singing, Gates has flipped.
Kellyanne, back to your crypt.

March 10, 2018

<u>Headline</u>: Trump holds a rally in Pennsylvania for
Rick Saccone in advance of its Special Election.

PA election coming soon.
Another rally by the goon.
Lies-to-truth: no ratio.
More verbal felatio.
More hate, more bragging, it's his thing.
Who pulled Chatty Donny's string?
Donny, want a record turnout?
Resign, you vile, racist burnout.

March 11, 2018

Ode to a Failed Rally

Goodnight Twitter what's the tally
Of lies told at the moron's rally?
Still obsessed with Hillary.
It seems he cannot let her be.
Sick of all his racist yelling.
Lie-filled tweets with awful spelling.
Clearly every school did fail him.
Someone, please can you just jail him?

Song Break: To Simon & Garfunkel's The Sounds of Silence

Sitting watching FOX&Friends.
Wearing nothing but Depends.
They all know that Don Jr. lied
About the meeting he tried to hide.
Now the cries for impeachment
They echo through the Senate halls.
Justice calls.
I hear the sound of sirens.

And the people bowed and prayed.
For the country you betrayed.
Oh how Mueller will teach you.
Traitor Don they will impeach you.
You can tweet your drivel from your cell.
Go to hell.
You'll hear the sound of sirens.

March 13, 2018

Headline: Tillerson is fired via tweet after saying that Russia should face consequences for launching a nerve agent attack near London. Also, Trump calls for a "Space Force", a new division of the armed forces in space.

Goodnight Twitter, what a day.
Looks like Rex has gone away.
Cut by tweet by moron prez.
Why? Because Putin says.
Want more Trump disgrace?
Now he wants soldiers in space.
So bad an idea, it's hard to absorb it.
Hope they send Trump himself into orbit.

March 14, 2018

<u>Headline</u>: Reports surface that Don Jr. is divorcing.
In other news, Democrat Connor Lamb is
announced as the winner in a PA district that Trump
won by 20 points in 2016.

G'night Twitter. well of course
Traitor Tot heads for divorce.
Now it seems that Fredo had
Cheat on his wife like dear old dad.
In other news Saccone's loss
Shows Donnie is an albatross.
His rallies and his rambling words
Turn all they touch to orange turds.

March 15, 2018

G'night Twitter, O remorse
Traitor Tot heads for divorce.
Bet his cheating was a bore
Plus his gifts from the Trump Store.
His next wife: no discussion
Sure to be a migrant Russian.
One more import tale of woe
They Russian where wise won't go.

Song Break. To The Beatles A Little Help From My Friends

What do you do with an orange baboon
Who is racist and dumb as can be?
I have no fear Mueller will right this wrong.
He will charge Trump with a felony.
Trump hides it all on Fox&Friends.
He can lie to us on Fox&Friends.
He'll deny it all on Fox&Friends.

March 17, 2018

<u>Headline</u>: St Paddy's Day – Jeff Sessions fires Andrew McCabe, Trump boasts about the firing in a tweet, and again tweets that the Russia probe is a "witch hunt" (in caps lock, of course) based upon a "fake dossier".

G'night Twitter on St Paddy
Melting down is Orange Fatty.
Mar-a-Lard-Ass crying 'witch hunt'.
Just another whiny bitch stunt.
Mueller finds the tweetstorm pleasin'
Just more evidence of treason.
Whine on, Don, but they won't fail
To put your obese butt in jail.

Song break! To The Beatles When I'm 64

There is a dotard with orange hair
Not impeached somehow.
Everybody knows that treason is a crime.
Some day Donnie soon will do time.
Tweeting his nonsense in Donaldese.
God he's such a bore.
Speaks like an infant, acts like tyrant
I think Don is 4.

March 18, 2018

<u>Headline</u>: Trump tweets that the Russia probe must
end because "NO COLLUSION".

G'night Twitter, think you felt down?
Mar-a-Lard-Ass had a meltdown.
Kept on tweeting "NO COLLUSION!"
Donny thy name is Delusion.
Obstructing justice with each tweet.
Hang on all, and grab a seat.
His feed will lend to much excitement.
Tweets himself into indictment.

March 20, 2018

<u>Headline</u>: Tomi Lahren boasts of her "family, freedom and final thoughts" tour. Dear G-d help us all.

G'night Twitter, oh the barren
Mind of Fox's Ptomaine Lahren.
Says she is about to tour on
Quest to prove that she's a moron.
Tomi want a final thought?
Your IQ score's a perfect naught.

Song Break: To Bob Dylan's Blowing in the Wind:

How many lies can Donnie tell
Before Fox will say he's insane?
How much hair dye will they have to sell
To keep that combed-over orange mane?
The hairpiece my friend is blowin' in the wind.
The hairpiece is blowin' in the wind.

March 21, 2018

<u>Headline</u>: Trump, tweets that "special council"
never should have been appointed for the Russia
probe. It was not a typo, he repeated "council" 4
times over 3 more tweets.

G'night Twitter. Orange dullard
Tweet-slammed Special "Council" Mueller.
NO COLLUSION!, he may yell it.
But "counsel", sadly, he can't spell it.
If treason's too hard to explain
Can we impeach for lack of brains?
Stable Genius, beg your pardon.
But he could not pass kindergarten.

March 22, 2013

<u>Headline:</u> HR McMaster resigns or is fired as
National Security Advisor, Trump picks hawk John
Bolton to replace him. We're all going to die.

Goodbye peace, hello gloom.
FFS we all are doomed.
No fate could be as revoltin'
As Nat. Sec. Advisor Bolton.
War's a coming, better hunker
Down in an old air raid bunker.
Nuclear annihilation
May be better for the nation
Than living in this tire dump
Brought to bear by moron Trump.

Song Break: To Dire Straits' Walk of Life

Here come Donny with porn star Stormy
"Spank me Ivanka, honey, what'd I say."
Here come Donny
With the Frank Graham endorsement.
A model Christian, people watch him pray.

The Russian faction, the Putin notion.
Yeah, he'll do what they say.
He colluded. He's deluded
Please Mueller indict him we all pray.

He brags about groping a woman.
With STDs he probably he is rife.
Oh Donny cheats. he cheats on his wife.
Yeah he cheats on his wife.

March 24, 2018

<u>Headline</u>: The March For Our Lives

G'night Twitter g'night moon.
NRA you'll be out soon.
Students spoke, we heard their voices.
Come November, we have choices.
GOP can think and pray.
But we won't choose the NRA.
Schools will be a place for math,
Not arming every psychopath.
Election day is coming fast
NRA you're in the past.

<u>Headline</u>: March 24, 2018. After the March for Our Lives, NRA spokeswoman Dana Loesch records an NRATV video warning actors and the media that "their time is up" and "the clock starts now".

Song break! To Oh Xmas Tree

Oh Dana Loesch you psychopath.
It's you who'll be a goner.
You think these kids will go way
You couldn't be much wronger.*
You threaten stars & athletes
With shrill & psychopathic tweets.
When GOP lose Senate seats
You won't be in much longer.

*Poetic license on "wronger": It's not a word, I know, but if fit the rhyme and meter.

March 27, 2018

Headline: News reports claim that Trump is having a hard time finding a lawyer to defend him after John Dowd quit. Trump sends a tweet bragging that all lawyers want to represent him.

A Poem for Pro-Se President

G'night Twitter what a journey.
Trump has lost all of his attorneys.
With his raving he ran through them.
He's down to 800-SUE-THEM.
No attorney worth a whip.
Would go aboard that sinking ship.
Donny, boy you sure are screwed
Your firm now: Raip, Lye & Killude

Song Break To The Beatles Come Together

Here come ol fat slob, hair come unglued slowly.
He got tiny fingers.
He one orange moron.
He got hairpiece blowin free.
Think he's a dictator who can do as he please.

He knows no English.
Caps lock random letters.
He eat KFC and he down diet cola.
He don't know his ABCs.
Someone call his lawyer time to pay off Stormy.
Come on Mueller, right now, set us free.

March 28, 2018

<u>Headline</u>: Laura Ingraham mocks Parkland survivor
David Hogg for being rejected by UCLA despite a
4.2 GPA. He responds by asking her advertisers to
sever ties with her show, and they do, with 16
cutting ties with her show within 6 hours of his
tweet.

Gnight Twitter & it's been said
Oh I hate Laura Inbred.
Bullied David about college.
Oh Laura lacks in basic knowledge.
She forgot the voices rising
Cost her all advertising.
1st Amendment rights we call it.
Boycott all, #GrabYourWallet.

March 31, 2018, Ted Nugent and Frank Stallone
join in attacking the Parkland students.

Goodnight Twitter, I discern
NRA will never learn.
Has-been Nugent, dumb & vile
No more than a pedophile.
He can bully, gripe and yak.
We all know what they all lack
Stallone and Ted, just drop the meanness.
We promise: We'll buy each you a penis.

Song Break To Crosby Stills & Nash's Teach Your Children

You, you're a bloated load.
Your every meal consists of Big Macs.
Golf at our expense, with undue stress
Straining your golf slacks.
You just tweet and you deny.
But we know that you just lie.
And that's the reason why
They will impeach you.

April 1, 2018

Laura Ingraham thought she could trifle
With students she's trying to stifle.
But she's learning fast
She'll be out on her ass.
She'll be home now just buffing her rifle.

Song Break: To Hey Jude

"Fake News", tweets tiny hands
"It's a witch hunt" he'll whine and stammer.
A pile of barely literate mass.
Trump couldn't pass his grade school grammar.

"Fake News", he tweets each day.
It's his "I'm…in…deep…trouble" mantra.
For all his "there's no collusion" plea
All of us see: his Iran-Contra.

So, any time he sends a tweet,
You know he's beat.
He rants and he raves in his denial.
For well we know that he's insane.
He has no brain.
The KFC grease made him senile.
(na na na na nah).

Fox News is really bad.
But Trump's tweets are
Not that much better.
An angry, whiny, litany of lies
He can't disguise
WITH CAPS LOCKED LETTERS
LETTERS, LETTERS, LETTERS
LETTERS, LETTERS
Ahhhhhhhhh!
Na, na, na na, na na, na
Na, na, na, na, Fake News!

For the GOP

Goodnight Twitter, g'night moon.
GOP you're not immune.
Thoughts & Prayers are all you'll say.
You're owned by the NRA.
But you bastards one & all
Will be voted out next Fall.
The horror cannot be unseen
Of your damned AR 15.
If you won't ban it you'll see mobs
Vote each of you out of jobs.

Song Break! Oh Tomi
(Sung to Barry Mannilow's "Mandy")

Oh Tomi you speak & tweet without thinking.
You've got nothing to say
Oh Tomi you sound like Matt Gaetz
When he's been drinking.
Oh please go away.
Oh Tomi the bleach in your hair did not age well,
I'd go back to the store.
Oh Tomi it seems that it killed your last brain cell
You're an ignorant bore O Tomi.

April 9, 2018

<u>Headline</u>: Sara Palin says she'd like to run for
higher office again.

She governed an iceberg, two days on the job.
But point out that fact, "its Fake News," she'll sob.
Little experience to build her case on.
Ideals, to the right of good ol' Genghis Khan.
The schools will be shuttered, books will be burnin'
To welcome the day to say "goodbye to learnin".
Learnin's so tough! Books such a bore!
Who needs a globe—Russia's just out her door!
A pacifist really, kind and humane.
Shooting at wolves from the door of a plane
Guns in all schools? "It's a task from above,"
Said this pro-life assassin the GOP loves.
Guns are His Way, so we must see it through.
Let the body count climb it's what Jesus Would Do!
'Abortion is murder', planned parenthood scorned.
To her life is precious...until it is born.

Song Break: Song for Traitor Tot (Donald Trump Jr.), sung to Eric Clapton's Layla

What do you do when they have Comey?
You know how he testified.
You can tweet, but Traitor Tot, you're beat.
You lied to the FBI.
Fredo! It looks like you are caught.
Fredo! Your lies are all for naught.
Fredo! Cut a deal and clear your guilty mind.

Make the best of the prosecution
In your family, you're the clown.
Like a fool. you met with Russians too.
Now you all are going down.
Fredo! They'll have you on your knees.
Fredo! Your mind is so diseased.
Fredo! Cut a deal and save your pale behind.

It's Mueller Time

Hello Twitter, 'tis the season.
Dotard has committed treason.
To deflect from his conspirin'
He may soon commence the firin'.
But, Don the thing you think your fixin'
Didn't work too well for Nixon.
Fire and you'll meet his fate.
Disgraced, impeached for RussiaGate.

April 10, 2018

<u>Headline</u>: The FBI raids the home and office of
Trump's personal attorney, Michael Cohen.

The FBI has got a plan.
The borscht's about to hit the fan.
The Feds came in to raid the home.
Of Bugsy's lawyer, Michael Cohen.
Seems they don't think Stormy's payout
Was the lawyer's personal lay out.
Young and old will soon applaud.
If this was election fraud.
Trumpy, buckle up now, honey.
The Feds are following the money.

April 12, 2018

Headline: James Comey's book. A Higher Loyalty, detailing his meetings with Trump, is about to hit shelves. A preview expanded on Comey's testimony that Trump demanded an oath of loyalty, like a mafia don.

The Dimwit Don

Hello Twitter, Comey's book
Reveals that Trump is just a crook.
Demanded oaths of loyalty.
As if he came from royalty.
Donny is no Gotti, though
(His IQ is far too low).
If anyone, he's Putin's Fredo.
A step away from eating Play-doh.
The mob boss name for this dumb con
Could only be The Dimwit Don.

Song Break: To Rainbow Connection

Why are there so many tweets, 'No Collusion!'
What does Trump have to hide?
Each tweet's a lesson in rage & delusion.
But we all know Donnie lied.
What's so amazing
Is how he's stark raving
Treasonous, ignorant slime.
Mueller will find it
The Russia connection.
Then Don will be soon doing time.

For the Russia Probe

Trump always tweets "No Collusion!"
He seems to be suffering delusion.
For the crime, you see,
Is conspiracy.
Hence, the moron's confusion.

He thinks if just keeps on tweeting
They'll think that he hadn't been cheating.
If the GOP nation
Stops the investigation
Come elections, they'll all take a beating.

April 16, 2018

Headline: Sean Hannity is revealed as "Client No 3"
when a New York Judge orders Trump lawyer
Michael Cohen to reveal the identify of his mystery
client.

Ode to Sean Hannity

Hello, client No 3
Better known as Hannity.
Sean attacks the FBI.
Now we see the reason why.
Sean & Trumpy share a yen
For bedding porn stars now & then.
Smashed his Keurig in protest
What will he smash to quell this mess?

<u>Headline</u>: Hannity denies that he ever retained
Michael Cohen, despite admissions from Cohen's
attorneys that Hannity is, in fact, the mystery client.

G'night Twitter g'night moon.
Hannity, you dumb maroon.
Came as no surprise to me
To learn you're client # 3.
With all your anti-Mueller shows
Seems that you failed to disclose.
You are so Cohen/Trump compliant
Because you are the target's client
Can't wait for you to hope & pray.
Cohen, he has no NDA.

Song Break! To Light My Fire

Oh nothing Donnie says is true.
He's just a pathological liar.
Please Mueller say his reign is through.
The situation's getting dire.

With the Russians he conspired.
With the Russians he conspired.
Please someone impeach this liar!

We know his fate is up to you.
FoxNews is preaching to its choir.
What more does he have to do?
Who else will you let him fire?

With the Russians he conspired.
With the Russians he conspired
Please someone impeach this liar!

<u>Headline</u>: Comey's book is released. Trump has an epic twitter-tantrum meltdown.

Comey's book has hit the stores.
With tales of Donny and his whores.
And how Mike Flynn's known conspiring
Lead ol' Don to Comey's firing.
Now there is but one deduction:
Donny's guilty of obstruction.
He'll lie, and whine, and tweet and rail.
But Donny will end up in jail.

The Lyin' King

How do you tell when old Donnie is lying?
He's making a promise, or else, he's denying.
How do you tell Trump's lie when it comes?
His moving his lips, or maybe his thumbs.
How do you know when Trump's buried the lead?
Just read 'tween the lines of his Twitter feed.
How do you tell the real news from fake?
You know Trump is lying, cause he is awake.
Trump is the king of the Lies Hall of Fame.
With more awful lies than his constant golf game.
How do you know which version to choose?
Each word from his mouth or his thumbs is fake
news.

Song Break! To John Lennon's Imagine

Imagine Trump in prison.
It's easy if you try.
No caps locked tweeting,
Just treason rat, goodbye.
Imagine all Team Treason
Carted off in cuffs.
You may say I'm a dreamer.
But the moron's time has come.
Oh Mueller won't you join us.
And this nightmare will be done.

Imagine Trump indicted.
It isn't hard to do
No NDA would save him.
His Twitter rants were through.
Imagine Federal agents
Take him off in cuffs.
You may say I'm a dreamer
But Donny's pretty dumb.
He'll keep tweeting confessions.
And his lies will come undone.

Coda

Thank you all, who stopped by to read
Of the moron whose racism, ignorance, greed
Tries to destroy us with each tweeted letter
But together, we all can help make it better,
Get out the vote, with passion and verve.
Elect honest leaders that we all deserve.
Who'll make our world better, instead of worsen
By standing for equal rights for every person.
Vote for our future, for only then
Can we make America great once again.